Ft. Zumwalt West Middle School
150 Waterford Crossing
O'Fallon, MO 63366

GALAXY OF SUPERSTARS

98° Faith Hill
Ben Affleck Lauryn Hill
Jennifer Aniston Jennifer Lopez
Backstreet Boys Ricky Martin
Brandy Ewan McGregor
Garth Brooks Mike Myers
Mariah Carey 'N Sync
Matt Damon Gwyneth Paltrow
Cameron Diaz LeAnn Rimes
Leonardo DiCaprio Adam Sandler
Céline Dion Will Smith
Sarah Michelle Gellar Britney Spears
Tom Hanks Spice Girls
Hanson Jonathan Taylor Thomas
Jennifer Love Hewitt Venus Williams

CHELSEA HOUSE PUBLISHERS

Galaxy of Superstars

98°

Tim O'Shei

Chelsea House Publishers
Philadelphia

Frontis: Pictured from left to right are the guys of 98°—Nick Lachey, Drew Lachey, Jeff Timmons, and Justin Jeffre.

CHELSEA HOUSE PUBLISHERS

Editor in Chief: Sally Cheney
Associate Editor in Chief: Kim Shinners
Production Manager: Pamela Loos
Art Director: Sara Davis

Produced by
21st Century Publishing and Communications, Inc.
New York, New York
http://www.21cpc.com

© 2002 by Chelsea House Publishers, a subsidiary of Haights Cross Communications. All rights reserved. Printed and bound in the United States of America.

The Chelsea House World Wide Web address is
http://www.chelseahouse.com

First Printing

1 3 5 7 9 8 6 4 2

Library of Congress Cataloging-in-Publication Data

O'Shei, Tim.
   98° / Tim O'Shei.
      p. cm. — (Galaxy of superstars)
   Includes bibliographical references and index.
   Summary: A look at the lives of the individual members of the popular group, 98°, and at evidence of the group's success.
   ISBN 0-7910-6467-0 (alk. paper)
   1. 98 (Musical group)—Juvenile literature. 2. Rock musicians—United States—Biography—Juvenile literature. [1. 98° (Musical group). 2. Singers.]
   I. Title. II. Series.
   ML3930.A14 O84 2001
   782.42164'092'0—dc21

                                                                               2001032405

> *Dedication:* To Michelle & Cara. Thanks for your help; keep chasing your dreams! — T. O.

Contents

Chapter 1
Index Card Mania   7

Chapter 2
Ohio Boys   13

Chapter 3
Just Us in Hollywood   25

Chapter 4
Temperature Rising   35

Chapter 5
Revelation   47

Chronology   57
Accomplishments   58
Further Reading   59
Index   60

1

INDEX CARD MANIA

Jeff Timmons, Justin Jeffre, and Nick and Drew Lachey pulled themselves out of bed at 5 A.M. On the morning of May 24, 1999, in Minneapolis, Minnesota, the foursome known as 98° had a plane to catch. As the guys boarded their plane that morning, they were in for a rough ride because of a heavy rainstorm. But as a popular 98° song says, there's always "sunshine after the rain." And plenty of brightness was awaiting their arrival in western New York.

Jeff, Justin, Nick, and Drew were supposed to fly eastward to Buffalo, New York, where they would play a concert for over 1,000 teenagers at a suburban high school called Kenmore West. Usually, successful groups like 98° don't play shows in high schools. Concert halls, stadiums, and arenas are more common venues for pop groups, but this was a special concert. A popular Top 40 radio station in Buffalo, WKSE 98.5 FM, had run a contest called High School Spirit in which students from all over the area had to submit 3-by-5-inch index cards with their name, age, school, and phone number. The school that submitted the most cards would win a

---

In 1995, four young men from Ohio – Jeff Timmons, Justin Jeffre, Nick and Drew Lachey – formed the singing group 98°. They were the newest addition to the boy band craze in pop music.

free concert from 98°. Kenmore West was that lucky school. The school that came in second, Lewiston-Porter High School, would get a visit from the group.

The guys made it to Buffalo safely and were whisked away to Lewiston-Porter, which is located near Niagara Falls. The students at Lew-Port had submitted 1.4 million index cards, finishing second in the contest and earning a visit from the group. Shortly before 2 o'clock that afternoon, Jeff, Justin, Nick, and Drew showed up at the school. For about an hour they signed autographs, posed for pictures, and chatted with students, teachers, and school staff.

Meanwhile, classes had ended at Kenmore West High School, located about a half-hour away, and students were piling into the auditorium. For two hours, 1,400 students waited patiently, many of them carrying handmade signs. Everyone was ready for 98°.

Over the four weeks of the School Spirit contest, Kenmore West's students had submitted 1.8 million index cards. In total, WKSE had received 14.9 million cards. "We can't move around here," program director Dave Universal said during the contest. "Every day kids come into the lobby with boxes of more cards. We've never had this kind of response before. It's out of control."

Kids from all around western New York had spent hours each day filling out cards. Office supply stores couldn't keep up with the demand for index cards. For weeks, index card mania was the biggest craze in Buffalo . . . and it was all for 98°. That's why the band was so determined to thank its fans by putting on a super concert. "We think this is a great contest,"

INDEX CARD MANIA

Justin had said in an interview on the station's morning show.

Every night during the contest, teenagers would call WKSE's evening disc jockey, D. J. Anthony, and tell him how their classmates were teaming up to win the contest. "It was incredible, just wild for 98°," Anthony said. "The whole town had come together with the index cards. People put a lot of time in and it brought a lot of families closer together. It brought a lot of friends close together: People had pizza parties, sleepovers, and everything else. 98° was just super-duper pumping."

By the time the group reached Kenmore West shortly after 4 o'clock, they were touched by how much adoration they had received from their fans. That reception made Jeff think about how much good 98° was doing

98° started out promoting their first hit, "Invisible Man," in small venues such as malls and fairs. Soon, the band would be embarking on an international tour, which would give them a huge fan base.

with its music. Those 14.9 million index cards were the result of students in every school coming together to work on a project. They had set a goal and used hard work and teamwork to chase after it. That's exactly what Jeff, the guy who had started 98° four years earlier, had done to help the group to reach the top. From inside his dressing room in Kenmore West, Jeff could see just how true his dream had become. "That they would turn in that many cards to see us is amazing," Jeff told a reporter from the Buffalo News. "We're completely flabbergasted."

The 98° contest came at a time when people all across America were questioning school spirit and the effect of music on kids. In a small but important way, this school concert was a reminder that music can be uplifting and even inspire kids to come together and work for something good. "We're honored to be here," Justin said. "With all the recent trouble high schools across the country are having, it's a wonderful thing to see something positive like this."

Shortly before 5 o'clock—12 hours after they awoke halfway across the country—98° was introduced to the Kenmore West crowd by D. J. Anthony. "The vibe was awesome," he remembered. "When we came up to the school, people were just dying for us to come on in. When 98° took the stage, of course, the [crowd went] crazy."

For the next 35 minutes, amidst the screams and cheers, Jeff, Justin, Nick, and Drew put on the most memorable show to ever grace that stage. Dancing in their black and white outfits, they sang three of their most popular songs: "Invisible Man," "The Hardest

Thing," and the tune with the most fitting lyrics of the day, "All Because of You":

You're my sunshine after the rain.

You're the cure against my fear and my pain . . .

Despite the early and stormy start to their day, 98° had brought the sunshine to Buffalo. To make music so powerful that an entire city would run out of index cards was a long way to come for the group. Just a few years earlier, the four guys were working as delivery boys and security guards, sleeping in a cramped apartment with a mattress pulled from the garbage. To get people to listen to them, they had to stand on the sidewalk and sing for hours.

Things were different now, and they could see that as Buffalo was overtaken by 98° fever. Within the next couple of years, the rest of the country would follow: 98° would only get hotter and hotter.

2

OHIO BOYS

Justin Jeffre always wanted to be a rock star. Singing was his dream . . . but he had a backup plan. "If that didn't work out too well," he wrote in a question/answer session on the official 98° website, "I wanted to be a cowboy." In any case, Justin's first choice worked out fine.

The son of Susan and Dan Jeffre, Justin Paul Jeffre was born on February 25, 1973, in Mount Clemens, Michigan, and raised in Cincinnati, Ohio. He has an older brother (Dan), a younger half-sister (Alexandra), and two stepsiblings (Ann and Jeff).

As a kid, Justin's biggest passion was music. He loved listening to R&B artists like James Brown, Otis Redding, and Stevie Wonder. Sometimes on Sundays, Justin would go to a Baptist church with a friend simply to hear the choir.

Justin attended a private elementary school. When he was 11 years old, he spent a day with his cousin Stella at her school, the Cincinnati School for Creative and Performing Arts. He liked it so much that he auditioned with hundreds of other kids. Among the things Justin

---

Of the four band members, Jeff Timmons was only one who did not grow up in Cincinnati. Justin, Nick, and Drew all attended the Cincinnati School for Creative and Performing Arts.

Originally a drama major at the Cincinnati School for Creative and Performing Arts, Justin quickly switched to music. He and fellow 98° member Nick Lachey performed in a barbershop quartet and a doo-wop/soul band called the Avenues.

had to do was act like a hot air balloon, so he puffed up his cheeks and stuck out his arms. Justin must have been a good hot air balloon, because he was one of only 10 kids picked.

At Performing Arts, Justin started getting a sense that something special was in his future. "It was a gut feeling," he said on MTV. "From the seventh grade, I used to pray about it. I always believed that if you really wanted something and worked hard toward it, you could realize it."

Justin started as a drama major, but quickly switched to music. He practiced his vocal skills and learned to play the trombone. At family gatherings, Justin would often belt out a tune or put on an improvised skit. At school, he was always looking for opportunities to get involved and chase his dream. He met Nick Lachey at school one day when he heard a group of students singing a cappella (with no instrumental accompaniment). The songs were by a gospel group named Take 6. A big fan of Take 6, Justin walked into the room and learned that the guys were rehearsing for a tribute show to Dr. Martin Luther King Jr. Justin got involved and, through that show, became friends with Nick.

Over the next few years, Justin and Nick sang together in a barbershop quartet, an oldies group at King's Island amusement park in southern Ohio, and a doo-wop/soul band called the Avenues, in which both guys played horn and performed vocals. Typically, Justin helped Nick get involved in those groups.

The ironic thing about all this is that when he wasn't performing, Justin was actually a shy kid. He would sit in the back of the class and hardly participate. "I used to be one of the shyest people you would ever meet," he told *16* magazine. "But as I got older I found that it's important to live life to the fullest and don't be afraid to make a fool of yourself and have fun."

After high school, Justin went on to the University of Cincinnati, where he majored in history. He performed on the weekends, but not nearly as much as he had in high school. One day that changed when he received an irresistible offer from his old buddy Nick.

It had been Justin who had helped Nick get a few singing gigs in high school. Now, Nick was about to return the favor. The rest of that story comes later.

Unlike Justin, Nick didn't spend his childhood days dreaming of a recording career. Nick loved sports and was a big Cincinnati Bengals fan. He would have liked to grow up and play football for the team. But Nick was a competitive kid, which is what led him into show business. When Nick was 12, his 9-year-old brother Drew auditioned for the Cincinnati School for Creative and Performing Arts. Drew was accepted and the Lachey family made a big deal about it.

"The only reason we even went to the same school was because my whole family was bragging and talking about how proud they were of Drew for getting in," Nick told *People* magazine in an interview with the brothers. "Blah, blah, blah. I got sick of hearing about it. So I went down and auditioned too. I had no intention of going. I just wanted to prove I could get in."

Drew chimed in, "He had to steal my thunder."

After singing "My Country 'Tis of Thee," doing a drawing, writing a story, and acting like he was sneaking up on and scaring someone, Nick passed his audition. He ended up attending seventh grade at the school and found he liked it. With that, young Nick's goals turned to music. It was a move that one-day would lead to stardom.

Nicholas Scott Lachey was born on November 9, 1973, in Harlan, Kentucky, to Cate Fopma-Leimbach and John Lachey. Around the time he learned to walk, the family moved to College Hill, Ohio, on the outskirts

Nick Lachey began his singing career as a child in the church choir. In high school Nick was not only a talented singer but he played the saxophone and was a star football player.

of Cincinnati. Nick's parents divorced when he was in first grade, and the boys lived with their mom. "She taught us, 'Seize your opportunities now. Decide what you really want to do, then just go for it and enjoy what you're doing,'" Nick told the *Cincinnati Enquirer*.

Both Nick and Drew have always been close to their dad, too. Growing up, they lived near him and saw him all the time. "I have a real loving family, and even after the divorce my dad never lived more than five minutes away from me," Nick said in *98°: The Official Book.* "He was always there for Drew and me, and we were always well loved and well taken care of."

With that support, Nick had full freedom to pursue all the opportunities he wanted in school. He was a regular in musicals, playing the Cowardly Lion in "The Wizard of Oz" and Frederick in "The Sound of Music." Having begun his singing career as a child in the church choir, Nick kept it going at Performing Arts. He also played a mean saxophone and was a star football player in high school.

After graduation, Nick moved to Los Angeles to study Theater Arts at the University of Southern California. Nick had to leave Los Angeles and move back home for his second year of college because of money problems. So he enrolled in Ohio's Miami University and began studying sports medicine, reverting to his first love—athletics.

Andrew John Lachey was born on August 8, 1976, in Cincinnati. He is the second oldest in a large family. (Drew and Nick have a stepsister, Josie; half-brother, Isaac; and adopted siblings, Zac, Kaitlin, Sally, and Timothy.) Some of his best memories, he says, are of the trips he used to take with his grandparents. "We would pile into their motor home and just go all over," he told the Asian magazine *Teen Trends.*

One memory Drew will never forget is of his first bicycle at age 6. Not quite understanding how to work the brakes, Drew drove down a hill and couldn't stop. He almost crashed into a group of people but instead ended up in a lake!

Football, soccer, and gymnastics were among

When 98° needed a fourth member to complete the group, Nick called his younger brother Drew Lachey, who was working as an EMT in New York City. A baritone who was also trained at the Cincinnati School for Creative and Performing Arts, Drew fit right in.

the sports Drew participated in when he was young. Performing was in his mix of talents, too: As a kid, he was skilled at doing imitations of the dwarf Dopey from "Snow White." He also perfected his skills as a percussionist while attending school at Performing Arts.

Drew's mom Cate was a huge music fan, a love that rubbed off on him. Like his mom, Drew was a big fan of Marvin Gaye, the Temptations, and Stevie Wonder, among others. He had thought about trying to make performing a career, but late in high school Drew opted to leave the stage behind and build a career as an emergency medic.

Drew's interest in medicine was slightly different than Nick's. After Drew graduated from Performing Arts, he joined the army. His first goal was to become a fighter pilot, but later Drew decided that he would rather be a search and rescue worker, climbing cliffs to recover lost hikers in the Rocky Mountains. First, he needed to be certified as an emergency medical technician (EMT). After basic training in the army, Drew received medic training and became a certified EMT.

After receiving his certification, Drew joined the army reserves and moved to Brooklyn, New York, to begin his career as an EMT. He thought that getting experience in an emergency medicine job in a rough city like New York would increase his chances of getting a search and rescue job later. That was characteristic of Drew: Setting a goal, then working step-by-step to achieve it.

As it turns out, Drew followed his older brother into the spotlight. However, he's still keen on helping people. In the late 1990s, when 98° was touring cheerleading camps, Drew performed CPR on a fan. He also once aided an ill woman on an airplane.

While Jeff Timmons's voice blends in well with his groupmates, he's different from them in many other ways. For one, Jeffrey Brandon Timmons is the only group member who didn't grow up in Cincinnati. Jeff was born on April 30, 1973, in Canton, Ohio, to Patricia and Jim Timmons. With his older brother Mike

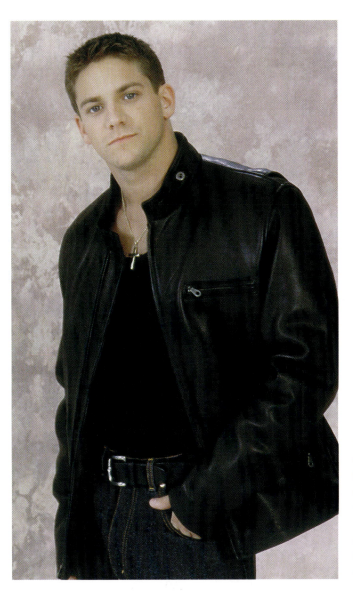

Jeff Timmons discovered a hidden talent for singing while in college. Intent on pursuing a singing career, Jeff moved to Los Angeles and recruited the current members of 98° for his group.

and younger sister Tina, Jeff was raised in Massillon, a northern Ohio city of 31,000 people that is located close to the Pro Football Hall of Fame. Actually it was a career in football, not singing, that was Jeff's number one goal while growing up. He wanted to play in the National Football League. One of his fondest memories as a kid was meeting football legends O. J. Simpson, Joe Namath, and Roger Staubauch at the Hall of Fame.

Jeff is also the only member of 98° who has no formal voice training. He told *Tiger Beat*, "Most of the training I got vocally has been through this group." He hardly sang growing up, except for a bit in the school choir and several appearances in musicals. Jeff was a trumpet player, too. People could see his natural musical talent, but Jeff was more interested in pursuing a football career.

As a kid, Jeff showed the same dedication toward reaching his football goals as he would show later in life as a singer. He practiced throwing the ball, watched as many games as he could (especially those with the Dallas Cowboys), and played football straight through high school and into college.

Jeff was a popular kid in high school and won awards, including "Outstanding Freshman Boy" and, as a senior, "Prettiest Eyes." But Jeff also made his share of mistakes, too. He shared this story with *Teen* magazine: "I remember skipping school. My girlfriend had a car and once I cut school and I was driving her car in the afternoon. I stopped at a traffic light and my mum pulled up next to me, so she caught me."

When Jeff broke up with his girlfriend during his senior year, he was so depressed that he decided to study psychology in college so he could help people. While at Kent State University, Jeff majored in psychology and played football for Malone College. By now, Jeff had a pretty good idea that he wasn't going to make the National Football League. He was interested, however, in becoming a child psychologist or pediatrician, or maybe someday working as a lawyer.

Music? He hadn't thought about that as a career. That is, he hadn't considered it until his third year of college, when a simple request from some female friends sparked a series of events that would eventually build 98°.

3

JUST US
IN HOLLYWOOD

One day in his third year of college, Jeff Timmons not only impressed some friends, he also got himself started on a musical career. He just didn't know it at the time.

Jeff was at a party when some girls asked him and his buddies to sing. Jeff was up to the challenge. The guys went into a room and worked out some parts for the Temptations' classic "My Girl." Moments later, the guys—led by Jeff—sang the song. The girls were amazed at Jeff's smooth, strong voice. Jeff had always known he could sing, but he didn't realize how impressive his voice could be. Jeff began to consider that he might have a career as a performer.

In 1995, Jeff left Kent State University and moved to Los Angeles, where he rented a small apartment. Jeff pursued some acting jobs, and he was successful, landing roles in commercials, including a spot for the United States Navy. But Jeff's true love was singing, and he wanted to follow that dream. He put together a quartet of guys to form a vocal group he called "Just Us." But most of the guys in the original group were school friends of Jeff, and

---

The members of 98° all took different paths to stardom. Talent, instinct, and determination were key to making the guys a successful singing group.

they just didn't take it as seriously as he did. Jeff had visions of hit songs with sweet harmonies, and he was willing to work hard to make that happen.

"When we first started the group with some of my friends I went to high school and college with, I don't think they had the same idea about it as I did," Jeff told *Star Profile*.

> I was a little bit more serious than them. I had some goals I wanted to achieve, certain things I had in mind that I wanted to attain with the group. I think the other guys were less serious about it. They wanted to do it for fun. They wanted it a lot quicker, and they wanted to work a lot less to do the things necessary to get where we needed to go. It was just difficult. It is hard to find people that have faith and trust and dedication to do something in the arts.

To find singers who would be the right fit, Jeff placed ads in the newspaper. He auditioned several would-be members but didn't find anyone whose voice was the right fit for Just Us. Finally, one of his groupmates, Jonathan Lippmann, suggested that Jeff audition Jonathan's friend from high school at the School for Creative and Performing Arts in Cincinnati.

That friend's name was Nick Lachey. The only problem was that Nick was living in Ohio.

Jeff overcame that problem by interviewing Nick over the phone. Nick sang "In the Still of the Night" for Jeff, who knew right away that this was his guy. But Nick wasn't jumping at the chance to join the group right away, not over the phone at least. He wanted to hear Jeff

JUST US IN HOLLYWOOD

Nick Lachey works the crowd at the 1st Annual Nickelodeon Kids Music Festival. The group's high-energy performances endear them to fans all over the world.

sing. So Jeff and Jonathan belted out a Boyz II Men song.

Now Nick was intrigued . . . but he still wasn't convinced. He had been studying sports medicine at the University of Miami in Ohio and had to make a difficult decision: Should he leave college, move to Los Angeles, and pursue a career in music? Or should he do the safe thing—stay in college, earn his degree, and get a job? After a couple of days, and with the encouragement of his parents, Nick decided to take the risk and move to Los

Angeles. After all, he could always go back to college if music didn't work out.

When he met with Jeff and Jonathan in California, Nick suggested that Jeff get in touch with another friend from Cincinnati, a bass singer named Justin Jeffre. Though he had been enjoying college, Justin hadn't quite let go of his dreams of performing, either. He kept thinking back to New Kids on the Block, a boy band that was popular when he was a teenager. "I remember thinking, if those guys can do it, then I can do it and my friends can do it," Justin later told *Billboard*. "And that's what I wanted to do. I kept plugging away." Soon, Justin was living in Southern California and was part of the group, too.

The four guys began practicing hard every day, memorizing songs and perfecting their harmonies. Los Angeles is a city crowded with performers, so the competition for gigs was tight. But the guys of Just Us knew they had a special talent and were determined to be successful. Being big-time sports fans, the guys were eager to sing the national anthem for the Los Angeles Dodgers baseball team. They recorded a demo tape of the national anthem and sent it to the executive in the Dodgers office who was in charge of booking singers for games. They were told that there were no more openings available that season.

At first the guys decided to just try for basketball season with the NBA's Lakers or Clippers. But then they thought about baseball again, and decided to push their case a little. They planned to go to Dodger Stadium and sing on the sidewalk outside the office.

So one afternoon, Nick, Jon, Justin, and Jeff went to Dodger Stadium and just started

singing on the sidewalk. Their public performance attracted a bit of a crowd, including many people who worked for the Dodgers. At first, the booking executive wouldn't come out of her office. Eventually she did, and after listening to the guys in person, told them that they sounded good. A few days later, they got a call inviting them to sing before a game that weekend. The guys had a few dates to choose from, and they picked a game versus the Cincinnati Reds, their hometown team.

With their full-body fire suits and silver chest protectors, the members of 98° opened their "Heat It Up" tour in the spring of 1999. They performed all their hit songs plus re-makes of other popular songs.

"It was pretty amazing," Nick told *Star Profile*. "They had told us no. On one hand we said, 'Okay, let's just try for basketball season or whatever.' Then we said, 'You know what? Forget it. Let's just go down there and sing for people. What can it hurt?' We've tried to do that with everything we've done. Just go at it 100 percent and make things happen for yourself."

Chasing after their goals—even if their strategy was unusual at times— turned out to be a good idea for the guys. Especially when the wildly popular Boyz II Men came to town.

The guys in Just Us admired Boyz II Men, an R & B group known for its perfectly blended harmonies. They had tickets to a Boyz concert in Los Angeles one night, but Nick and Jeff didn't want to go. There was a football game on television, and they wanted to stay home and watch that instead. But Justin and Jonathan convinced them to go because they had a plan. Four years earlier, in 1992, Boyz II Men had been discovered by sneaking backstage at a New Edition concert and singing a cappella for the group. Impressed, one of the New Edition singers helped Boyz get a recording deal with Motown. Two years later, they were music superstars.

The four members of Just Us wanted to do the same thing. At the concert, they walked up to the security guard and asked to be let backstage. The guard, of course, said no. The guys persisted, and started singing to the guard. Their a cappella music didn't impress the security man much, but it did catch the attention of a local radio disc jockey who was hosting a party for some fans backstage. The disc jockey asked the guys to come back and sing for the partygoers backstage. She even put them live on KBBT 92.3 FM radio in Los Angeles. Just Us had made the airwaves.

Jeff, Justin, Nick, and Jonathan didn't get to meet Boyz II Men before the show, so they slipped backstage *again* afterward. A man who had heard them sing earlier that night asked what they were looking for. When the guys said they wanted to meet Boyz II Men, the man told them that the group was already on its way out of the building. Then he introduced himself as Paris D'Jon, a music manager with a company called Top 40 Entertainment. D'Jon was the promoter for singer Montell Jordan, and he told the guys that he would like them to call him.

They did. Not long after, D'Jon helped them record demo songs in professional studios with top producers. D'Jon's first goal for the group was to get them signed with a record label.

Things were getting better, but there was still no sure promise of success. Jonathan Lippmann, who had brought Nick to the group, decided that he was ready to move onto other things. He wanted to build an acting career, and he told the guys he was leaving Just Us.

Suddenly, Jeff found himself back in his old situation: He needed another singer fast. D'Jon had booked Just Us at the Los Angeles House of Blues to open for Montell Jordan. The show would be a big step up for the guys. Nick told Jeff about his younger brother, Drew, who was working as an EMT in New York City. Drew had also attended the Cincinnati School for Creative and Performing Arts and was a baritone, like Jonathan. Nick contacted Drew, who wasn't sure he wanted to give up his life in New York to move west and sing, and convinced him to join.

The year 1999 was an amazing year for 98°. The group released 2 CDs with many hits and performed concerts all over the world.

    Drew needed to get to Los Angeles right away, so Nick booked an airline ticket and flew to New York to get Drew. Once there, he helped Drew pack and the brothers drove across the country, straight to Los Angeles. The three-day car ride gave Drew time to learn the parts for the House of Blues performance. Nick had brought along cassette tapes of demo songs the group had recorded, so they played them in the car and sang along. By the time the Lachey boys arrived in Los Angeles, Drew knew all his parts. He just didn't know his other groupmates. Nick introduced his brother to Jeff and

Justin, and right away the foursome began singing.

The House of Blues performance—the group's highest profile gig yet—was only two days away. Drew didn't have time to unpack; he had to practice. Although the group was under pressure, all four guys realized immediately that Drew's voice blended perfectly. A few nights later, at the House of Blues, Drew and his new groupmates turned in an amazing performance: It was clear that with Drew, Just Us was complete.

That was in November 1995. Over the next six months, the four guys lived together in a small Hollywood apartment and practiced their music every day. They held part-time jobs: Jeff delivered Chinese food, and Nick made pizza. Nobody had a lot of money. Drew and Nick actually slept on a mattress that the guys pulled from the side of the road.

During this time, they also found out that they needed a new name since the name "Just Us" was copyrighted by someone else. They picked 98° because they felt it represented body heat and passion, just like their steamy love songs.

Everything was set, except for one thing: 98° needed a record contract. This would come soon, but from the most unexpected of places.

4

TEMPERATURE RISING

The guys of 98° had dreams of reaching stardom. But only in their wildest fantasies did they imagine getting called to the Motown Records office.

That's exactly what happened in April 1996. Motown's new president, Andre Harrell, had just listened to the 98° demo that D'Jon had put together. Within days, the group was in his office, singing and dancing. After a few songs, Harrell was convinced. He told the guys, "I want to sign you."

Getting a recording deal was a big enough event, but having one with Motown was simply unbelievable for Jeff, Justin, Nick, and Drew. Motown was a legendary label in the music business. It was home to some of the most famous groups ever, including the Temptations, whose song "My Girl" is the one that got Jeff thinking about singing professionally. The Jackson Five, the 1970s group that included pop legend Michael Jackson, were Motown artists. So was Stevie Wonder, a vocalist who the entire group idolized. Even Boyz II Men was a Motown group. Something else was surprising, too. One thing that all Motown groups had in common, besides great singing, was that they were all were African

---

98° kicked off their first world tour in 1997, visiting Canada, Europe, and Asia. Here they are pictured in front of the Cinderella Castle at EuroDisney.

American. 98° was one of the first white groups signed to Motown.

Shortly after their signing, the group began working on its first CD, which eventually would be called simply *98°*. They worked in Los Angeles and traveled to New York and Atlanta to record the CD. It was released in the summer of 1997, highlighted by the single "Invisible Man." "I thought it was a great song," says Dave Universal, program director of WKSE-FM 98.5, a popular Top 40 radio station in Buffalo. "I didn't even know who they were, or care, to be honest with you. It was just a great . . . song [with a great hook] that I knew would be a hit."

Universal was right: "Invisible Man" was a hit, reaching number 12 on the *Billboard* charts. The song also became 98° first video, which was shot in a loft apartment that was part of an old factory in the SoHo section of New York City. The guys got a couple of their friends into the shoot, which shows a dance party. "We had this great song," Drew said on "Heat It Up," the group's official video, "and nobody really knew who we were."

Seeing the guys work in a city atmosphere was part of what Motown wanted to do with 98°. Harrell and other Motown executives wanted to do a few things to change 98° image to that of streetwise city boys. Jeff told *Entertainment Weekly:*

> They told us they wanted us to move to New York.
>
> When we said we didn't want to, they said, 'Don't move, and your record won't come out.' So we get to New York, and they had this idea that we were country

bumpkins, so they wanted us to hang with an urban crowd, get a lot of urban gear. You have a certain amount of faith that the record company knows what they're talking about, so we're like, 'Okay, maybe this is artist development.'

Motown was trying to create an image for its talented young artists. They wanted to mold 98° to fit in with a label that traditionally carried African-American artists. When 98° was first signed, the guys were reportedly told to lie about their ages to appear about four years younger. (That idea lasted about a week: The guys kept mixing up their fake ages.) Another thing Motown asked 98° to do was find a choir to join at a church in Harlem, an African-American section of New York City. "I wanted them to understand [African-American] culture and not just mimic it," Harrell told *Entertainment Weekly.*

That plan didn't work, either. The guys found a church in the phone book and went there one Sunday morning. The first thing they saw was yellow police tape around the building next door. In the church, the pastor started praying for people who had died the previous evening in a gambling hall. For four Ohio boys, it wasn't a comfortable place to be. "We're like, 'What are we doing here?'" Drew remembered. The guys didn't go back to that church.

The good news was that 98° wouldn't have to spend much time in New York. The guys went on a summer 1997 tour of the United States to promote "Invisible Man," traveling to cheerleading camps, malls, fairs, and other small venues. Getting their name and music

In April 1996, the group's biggest wish came true. Motown Records offered 98° a recording contract. They went on to release their first CD in the summer of 1997, *98°*.

out there was the goal: 98° traveled in a bus painted on the side with a larger-than-life picture of the group. To grab people's interest, they would take the bus through a town, tossing out free pictures, T-shirts, and CDs.

The group got a warm reception in the towns they visited, but "Invisible Man" had been released around the same time as the more-popular Backstreet Boys' hit "Quit Playing Games (With My Heart)." So 98° did something that many bands—including Backstreet Boys and 'N'Sync—found successful: They planned an international tour, visiting Canada, Europe, and Asia. The group built a huge fan base, especially among teenage girls. They came home that autumn knowing that their music was wildly popular outside of the United States.

Music groups measure their success by how many records they sell and by how many enthusiastic fans greet them at tour stops. To a respectable degree, 98° was successful on both counts. Another measure of success is having two or more popular singles from one album. They hadn't achieved that yet. Only "Invisible Man," from their first recording, reached hit status. But this problem was about to be solved.

While touring Asia, Jeff, Justin, Nick, and Drew learned that they would get a chance to record a song for the soundtrack of the upcoming Disney animated movie, *Mulan.* Working with 98° to record a song called "True to Your Heart" would be Stevie Wonder, the singer/songwriter, pianist, and harmonica player who began his career as a child. (The guys can give Nick some credit for suggesting the partnership with Wonder. When Nick heard part of the song before it was recorded, he told Motown that it sounded like a good Stevie Wonder tune.)

All four of the guys—especially Justin—had grown up admiring Wonder's work on songs like "I Just Called to Say I Love You" and "Superstition." They were looking forward to meeting him, but that didn't happen right away. The guys came home from Asia early and recorded their parts of the song, and then they returned to Asia to finish their tour. Wonder, meanwhile, recorded his parts separately. The producers then did what is commonly done in the industry: They put the tracks (different parts of the song) together, added in instrumentals and any sound effects, and produced a polished "final copy" of the song.

"I'll never forget the day that we got a copy of the finished project," Nick said on the group's official behind-the-scenes video "Heat It Up."

> I put it in the tape [player] and listened to it with my family. Seeing the expression on my parents' faces I think was even more rewarding to me than any personal satisfaction I got out of it. He's someone that they've grown up listening to and admire as an artist. It was so astounding to them to know that their son was singing with Stevie Wonder, and that really made me feel good.

The group finally met Wonder at the video shoot for the song in Hollywood. The video shows Wonder and 98° dancing and singing on a set resembling New York's Chinatown. The guys finally got to hang out and sing with Wonder. Jeff, Justin, Nick, and Drew met their hero, and he invited them into his trailer—where he had a keyboard—for an impromptu jam session. "During the video shoot he had us in his trailer, and he invited us to hang out there," Nick told music writer Rick Bird of the *Cincinnati Enquirer.* "He was playing the keys, we were just vibing and hanging out and singing."

Recording "True to Your Heart" gave 98° a great boost for their second album, *98° and Rising,* which they began work on in early 1998. The guys were very involved in the production of that album: Jeff had talked to

Motown's new president, George Jackson, and had been granted permission for 98° to help write, choose, and produce songs for the album, which would be released in October 1998. The group wrote half of the songs and worked closely with a team of top producers to get exactly the sound they wanted. Among the famous producers who helped with the album are Pras (from the Fugees), the Trackmasters (who have worked with Mariah Carey, Will Smith, and Mary J. Blige) and Anders Bagge (who has produced hits for Ace of Bace and Robyn).

Recorded in four cities over a two-and-a-half month time period, *98° and Rising* smashed the charts. The song "Because of You" reached number three on the *Billboard* charts, while "The Hardest Thing" broke the Top 20, too. Between the movie, video, and radio play, "True to Your Heart" was nominated for a Grammy, and "I Do (Cherish You)" became another popular song.

Five videos were filmed of songs from *98° and Rising:* "True to Your Heart," "I Do (Cherish You)" (which in a poll on the official 98° website, over 50 percent of fans picked as their favorite), "Because of You," "The Hardest Thing," and a live performance of "Heat It Up," a song cowritten by Nick.

These videos gave the guys a chance to show off their acting skills. (Remember, one of Jeff's early jobs was acting in commercials, and the rest of the guys were trained in drama at the Cincinnati School for Creative and Performing Arts.) In the video for "The Hardest Thing," Nick plays a boxer in Las Vegas, which required him to take lots of weightlifting training. In "Because of You," the group is shown singing atop the Golden Gate Bridge in San Francisco. That's no visual illusion: They really were standing on top of the 746-foot-tall bridge, where the wind was blowing at 50 miles per hour. Jeff, who is afraid of heights, had the toughest time with the shoot.

But then, 98° was getting accustomed to rising to high places. With the success of their second CD and their visibility on MTV and VH-1, they launched a North American tour in the spring. On their "Heat It Up" tour, the guys opened each show wearing full-body fire suits. Jeff, Justin, Nick, and Drew each emerged from a human-sized plastic tube with a sliding front door. Surrounded by smoke and echoed with cool sound effects, they moved in perfect synchronization and removed their masks, hoods, and fire jackets. Wearing silver chest protectors, they began singing and dancing. They performed all their hits songs plus their versions of other popular songs, including Offspring's "Pretty Fly (for a White Guy)" and Eminem's "My Name Is."

In the summer of 1999, 98° headlined the Nickelodeon All That Music & More Festival, traveling the country with acts such as Monica, Tatayana Ali, B*Witched, and Aaron Carter. With the tour, Justin, Nick, and Drew finally got to perform in their hometown, Cincinnati, for the first time. "We're definitely pumped up for that," Justin told the *Cincinnati Enquirer.* "It's great to finally come home and do a big show." Justin also admitted that with 98° two biggest teen music rivals (Backstreet Boys and 'N'Sync) having been created through auditions by producer Lou Pearlman in Orlando, he often found

With Motown President George Jackson at a plaque presentation for *98° & Rising*, the group's second album, which topped the charts after it's release in late 1998.

himself reminding people that 98° was a self-made band from the Midwest: "We tell people a lot, 'We aren't from Orlando; we are from Ohio.'"

By the first half of 1999, 98° had undergone a big change that few fans may have noticed. They were no longer with Motown Records. Two big recording companies—PolyGram (which owned Motown) and Universal—had merged into one company. While the business move was being made, 98° decided that Universal Records would be a better fit for their group, so they made the switch.

Over the summer, the group recorded its third album, *This Christmas*. The 11-song CD includes well-known favorites such as "Little Drummer Boy" and "The Christmas Song (Chestnuts Roasting on an Open Fire)." The disc also has original songs, such as "Christmas Wish," which Jeff wrote and produced on his laptop computer to make the sample recording.

98° headlined the Nickelodeon All That Music & More Festival in the summer of 1999. Their next album, *This Christmas*, was released in October 1999 by Universal Records.

This Christmas was released by Universal Records in October 1999, making it their third album in just over two years. After that release, the guys embarked on MTV's Fly2K worldwide tour, capping it off by cohosting the cable channel's New Year's 2000 party with actress Jennifer Love Hewitt. It topped off a busy year for Jeff, Justin, Nick, and Drew: In 1999, they had performed concerts all over the world, appeared on television talk shows, and promoted two CDs with lots of hits. Seemingly every time you flipped on a radio, or switched on a television, 98° was there. Their hard work gave people lots of music to enjoy, which was the group's gift to its fans.

Now, after two and a half years on the road, 98° was ready for some time off. That was their gift to themselves.

5

REVELATION

By the time the calendar hit 2000, Jeff Timmons, Justin Jeffre, and Nick and Drew Lachey had become true music stars. The CD *98° and Rising* had sold nearly five million copies, and *98°* and *This Christmas* had neared two million in combined sales. The group was recognized everywhere, largely because they had traveled to every part of the world.

The dream Jeff had when he moved to Hollywood five years earlier had come true many times over. But things weren't as pleasant as they might have appeared. Certainly, the guys were successful. But success brings a lot of extra pressures: For one, the group had parted ways in December 1999 with Paris D'Jon and Top 40 Management. Why? They can't say exactly, because the issue has gone to court. Nick offered this explanation to *Teen People* in September 2000: "We can't really discuss the situation in detail; it's not the appropriate time. It's safe to say that we felt hurt by a lot of things that happened in the last year concerning our management. I think our manner for conducting business differed greatly from his, and it's because of [this] that we made changes in our management."

By the year 2000, the members of 98° were true superstars. They had bona fide hits with their three albums *98°*, *98°and Rising*, and *This Christmas*. They were set to release their fourth album, *Revelation*.

Breaking with their manager was only one of 98° challenges at the end of 1999. After working so hard for so long, they were exhausted. "In between recording, promoting, and touring, we hadn't had any real time off in three years," Drew told *TV Guide.* "We were afraid to take even a day off because we didn't want to look back and say, 'If only we'd done that show.' But we'd reached a point where we were running on fumes."

The guys agreed to take a vacation from January to March. Each of them did something different: Jeff returned home to Los Angeles, where he has a home with his daughter Alyssa (who was born in early 1999) and her mother. Nick joined his girlfriend, pop singer Jessica Simpson, on her tour, and Drew and Justin each took warm-weather holidays: Drew to Mexico, Justin to the Caribbean.

When 98° regrouped in California a few months later to begin recording their fourth CD, the guys found that the break was the best thing they could have done. "I felt like this was the first time we got to catch our breath, get our creative vibe going and grow," Justin said in the official group biography from Universal Records. "We came back with fresh ideas and fresh ears. The hardest part of making this album was picking and choosing the songs, because there was a lot of material to choose from."

In making *Revelation,* the group was given almost full creative control. They could decide what kind of music they wanted, and they had an idea: It was time for 98° to make some dance music. "Every time we go to a club with music playing in the background, we never hear any of our stuff because it's too slow," Jeff told fans in a chat on *msn.com*. "So we wanted to make some music that would get people out of their seats and put that on the album."

While it still has plenty of the love ballads that are 98° trademark, *Revelation* isn't short on up-tempo tunes. The track, "Give Me Just One Night (Una Noche)" was originally created for pop star Ricky Martin. But the song's Swedish writers, Anders Bagge and Deetah, thought it was an even better fit for 98°. With a funky flamenco guitar beat and Latin feel, "Una Noche" broke new ground for 98°. "It's an up-tempo dance song," Nick told *launch.com*, "which is exciting for us because we've never had that out on radio before." (They also recorded a Spanish version.)

"Una Noche" became the first single from *Revelation*, getting released several weeks in advance of the CD. When the song was first sent to Top 40 radio stations on August 1, 2000, it set a record: 170 out of 172 possible stations added the song to their playlist. The video, which was shot on location in the midst of Mayan Ruins in Mexico, got lots of airplay on MTV. "Give Me Just One Night (Una Noche)" did exactly what 98° had hoped: It created lots of anticipation for the release of the *Revelation* CD on Tuesday, September 26, 2000.

To promote the release of *Revelation*, 98° launched a huge publicity campaign at the end of September. In the course of one week, they filmed a one-hour special for MTV's *First Listen;* appeared on *Total Request Live;* signed autographs at the Virgin Records Megastore at Times Square in New York City; had guest spots on *The Rosie O'Donnell Show, Live with Regis,* and *Good Morning America;* taped a radio special with New York's Z-100 FM that

The members of 98° sign autographs in New York City. "We really care about what our fans think," Nick told Carson Daly on *Total Request Live*.

was broadcast nationally; performed a private concert that was shown in Target stores nationwide; and conducted several online chats with fans.

The publicity push lasted well into the fall as the guys told interviewers and fans about their new mix of love ballads and dance tunes. "In the past, we've always been rushed to get albums done, for whatever reason, that we never had much say in it," Jeff told *J-14* magazine. "We'd always concentrate on the love songs first and we'd say we'll get to the up-tempos later. That would never come to fruition. This time, we've been fortunate enough to have more time to put the album together ourselves and really focus on the up-tempo tunes."

On MTV's *First Listen,* which first aired on Saturday, September 23, 2000, 98° told the stories behind the 13 songs on the CD, 11 of which they had written themselves. One of their favorites was "My Everything," a love song cowritten by Nick and Justin. It's a personal song, with lines such as, "Your spirit pulls me through.... When nothing else will do." Both men had their own reasons for writing the song.

"I wrote it for Jessica," Nick explained to *First Listen* host Brian McFayden, referring to Jessica Simpson.

"I like Jessica and all, but that wasn't my inspiration," Justin said with a chuckle. "We wrote it because we wanted it to be just a great love song. We wanted it to apply to a maybe spiritual relationship, a romantic relationship. Basically anything you wanted to apply it to, we want it to be able to do that."

Probably the most unusual song on *Revelation* is a punchy, electronically enhanced song called "Dizzy." Drew came up with the idea for the song after listening to the Goo Goo Dolls' CD titled *Dizzy Up the Girl.* He thought "dizzy" would be a cool concept for a song, and went to a small studio he has in his home and started to work on the idea. In the final version of the song, Nick actually does a rap. That's a huge leap from the love songs typical of 98°. "The rap was an experiment," Nick told *M* magazine. "I wrote it in five minutes."

Jeff, Justin, Nick, and Drew are never afraid to experiment. With the release of *Revelation,* they decided to explore a new way of getting fans involved in their career. Beginning with their appearance on *First Listen,* fans were invited to vote online for which song from *Revelation* should be the next single released. The voting on *mtv.com* began on September 23 and concluded on September 26. That day, 98° appeared on *Total Request Live* to announce the results with host Carson Daly.

The competition was tight between "My Everything" and a dance song, "The Way You Want Me To." The guys seemed to prefer "My Everything," probably because it had a lot of personal meaning to them. But they wanted their fans' opinion. "We really care about what our fans think," Nick told Carson on *Total Request Live.* "In terms of picking this next single, we really wanted to get their input." The results of the voting were extremely close. "My Everything" got 52 percent of the vote; "The Way You Want Me To" earned 48 percent.

When you listen to the music created by 98°, you could learn something about one of the guy's lives. Drew wrote "The Way You Do" for his girlfriend. "This a song about all the small little things a woman can do to touch your life, to make you really appreciate her," he said on *First Listen.* "This song was written for a special person in my life, and it's a testament to all the little things that make love a great thing."

When asked, Drew wouldn't name his girlfriend. He preferred to keep his relationship private. But less than a month later, he married her in a small, private ceremony in Cincinnati. It turns out that Drew's wife, whose maiden name was Lea Dellecave, is 98° choreographer. Along with designing dance routines for the guys, she has also danced with them onstage and in videos.

No reporters or television cameras were present at Drew and Lea's wedding. Privacy is something they cherish. Privacy sometimes suffers when you're a celebrity. Nobody knows that better than Nick, whose two-and-a-half-year relationship with Jessica Simpson was the cover story in magazines. Nick and Jessica met in December 1998 (they had the same manager at the time) and began dating shortly after. A few months into the relationship, they decided to go public and not try to hide it. "Everyone, from the press to our fans, [has] been really supportive," Nick told *M* magazine.

Jessica and Nick have even written songs together. Jessica has a song called "Where You Are," which is about dealing with the unexpected death of her cousin, Sarah. Nick shares vocals with Jessica in the song. "I definitely thought it had to be a duet," Jessica told *Seventeen* magazine. "When I heard Nick sing, I thought, 'He's got to do this.' I told him about Sarah, and he wrote his part."

Nick and Jessica chose to discuss their relationship publicly, but that would never work for Drew. "His relationship is in the spotlight, and I'd never want that," Drew told *YM*. "It makes me appreciate my own privacy." (In the spring of 2001, however, Drew and Lea were featured on a segment on the *Oprah Winfrey Show*.)

Though each guy has different preferences for his own privacy, they all appreciate how much fans will do for them . . . usually. Listening to their music, buying CDs, attending concerts, lining up for autographs, requesting their videos *on Total Request Live*—those are all good things. Some fans have taken their devotion further, such as getting 98° tattoos or, as a couple of girls did on *The Rosie O'Donnell Show*, baking a giant pretzel for the guys in the shape of a "98." Then there are other fans though who take things too far. "One time I came back from the gym at the hotel," Nick told fans in a chat on *alloy.com*, "and there were girls hiding under the laundry cart in the hall. They jumped out and started taking pictures!"

Things like that can get a little scary, but the group knows how much their fans love them. Before every performance, the guys say a quick prayer to thank God for the opportunity their fans have given them.

Sometimes, they still can't believe people find them so popular. "You never really get used to it," Drew told Rosie O'Donnell when she asked about girls screaming. "It's very flattering. I mean, we love it, obviously. But you never really quite get used it. It's like, 'Why are you screaming? It's us!'" They are still the same four guys from Ohio.

In August 2000 the guys returned to Cincinnati to film a concert special for the Disney Channel. "It's always been my dream to come home and have some kind of huge homecoming show," Nick told the *Cincinnati Enquirer.*

It was both a show and a tour. The guys took viewers on a tour of their hometown, visiting a Skyline Chili restaurant (a Cincinnati specialty) and a pizzeria, where Nick and Jeff tried to out-do each other in making pies. (Nick won.) The guys visited the training camp of the Cincinnati Bengals and played a touch football game with some players. They also sang the national anthem at a Cincinnati Reds baseball game and were honored by the mayor. Nick and Drew took viewers to their mom's house, which doubles as the headquarters of the 98° Worldwide Fan Club.

The group also visited Nick, Drew, and Justin's alma mater, the Cincinnati School for Creative and Performing Arts. They presented the school with a gift of $2,500, a grand piano, and several other instruments. Few people

realize how much 98° has done for the school: The presentation wasn't highlighted on the Disney special. "The band has quietly given quite a bit to their high school, but generally keep a pretty low profile when here in town," said *Cincinnati Enquirer* music writer Rick Bird, who has covered 98° entire career.

When these four guys found each other, the blend was so perfect that there was no stopping them. How long will 98° be around? That's up to the group. But if they want to keep making music, they're in a good position

98° released *Revelation*, their fourth album, in the fall of 2000. Before the album was released, the group had fans determine the release of their next single on *Total Request Live*.

to do so. The guys are at an age that appeals to both adults and teenagers. They've proven they can successfully perform both ballads and up-tempo music. They have the versatility to reach music-lovers everywhere.

"As long as they keep producing hits, they'll have some staying power," said Dave Universal, the program director from WKSE-FM in Buffalo. "This band could be around, potentially, for a long time. 98° doesn't have to be a boy band. 98° could just be the name of a band that's successful and pumps out hits."

That's exactly what 98° wants. "We want to make history," Nick said in the book *Bands We Love*. "Twenty years from now, I'd like to think 98° will leave a lasting impression."

CHRONOLOGY

1973	Justin Paul Jeffre born on February 25 in Mount Clemens, Michigan; Jeffrey Brandon Timmons born on April 30 in Canton, Ohio; Nicholas Scott Lachey born on November 9 in Harlan, Kentucky.
1976	Andrew John Lachey born on August 8 in Cincinnati, Ohio.
1995	Jeff Timmons moves from Ohio to Los Angeles to start a vocal group called Just Us; he is later joined by Jonathan Lippmann, Justin Jeffre, and Nick Lachey; Jonathan eventually leaves the group and is replaced by Nick's brother, Drew.
1996	After meeting music manager Paris D'Jon, the group—now called 98°—records a demo tape and is signed to Motown Records in April.
1997	The group's first CD, *98°*, is released in the summer; they go on their first tour to promote the album; "Invisible Man" reaches number 12 on the *Billboard* charts.
1998	The group continues touring; *98° and Rising* is released in October.
1999	Motown is bought out and 98° switches to Universal Records; group embarks on its Heat It Up tour and also headlines the Nickelodeon All That & More Music Festival; releases *This Christmas* in October; in December, 98° parts ways with Paris D'Jon and Top 40 Entertainment; the group finishes the year by participating in MTV's Fly2K worldwide tour.
2000	Jeff, Justin, Nick, and Drew vacation for the first three months, then begin recording their fourth album, *Revelation*, which is released in September.
2001	98° hits the road for a worldwide tour.

ACCOMPLISHMENTS

Albums (U.S.)

1997	*98°*
1998	*98° & Rising*
1999	*This Christmas*
2000	*Revelation*

Singles

1997	"Invisible Man"
1998	"Was It Something I Didn't Say" "Because of You"
1999	"Hardest Thing" "I Do (Cherish You)"
2000	"Give Me Just One Night (*Una Noche*)" "My Everything"

Videos

1999	*Kickin' It* (Unofficial) *Heat It Up* (Official)

FURTHER READING

Degnan, Lisa and Deborah Law. *Ninety-Eight Degrees.* New York: MetroBooks, 2000.

Furman, Leah & Elina. *The Heat Is on 98°.* New York: Ballantine Books, 1999.

Grabowski, John. *'N Sync.* Philadelphia: Chelsea House, 2000.

Nichols, Angie. *The Unofficial Book: 98°.* London: Virgin Books, 1999.

Sparks, Kristin. *98° And Getting Hotter!* New York: St. Martin's Press, 1999.

Squires, K.M. *98°: The Official Book.* New York: Pocket Books/Simon & Schuster, 1999.

Zier, Nina. *98° Backstage Pass.* New York: Scholastic, Inc., 1999.

Zymet, Cathy Alter. *Backstreet Boys.* Philadelphia: Chelsea House, 2000.

INDEX

"All Because of You"
(song), 11, 41
Backstreet Boys, 38, 42
Bagge, Anders, 41, 49
Bands We Love (book), 56
Billboard, 28
Boyz II Men, 27, 30,
31, 35
"Christmas Wish"
(song), 43
Cincinnati School for
Creative and Performing Arts, 13-15, 16, 18,
19-20, 26, 31, 41, 54-55
"Dizzy" (song), 51
D'Jon, Paris, 31, 35, 47
Entertainment Weekly,
36, 37
First Listen (television
show), 49, 50-51
Fopma-Leimbach, Cate,
16, 17, 19, 27, 40
"Give Me Just One
Night (Una Noche)"
(song), 49
"Hardest Thing, The"
(song), 10-11, 41
"Heat It Up" (song), 41
"Heat It Up" (video), 36,
40, 41
Heat It Up Tour, 42
"I Do (Cherish You)"
(song), 41
"Invisible Man" (song),
10, 36, 37, 38, 39
Jackson, Michael, 35
Jacksons, the, 35
Jeffre, Dan, 13

Jeffre, Justin Paul
birth, 13
childhood, 13-16
education, 13
as part of 98°, 33-56
joins Just Us, 28-33
Jeffre, Susan, 13
Just Us, 25-33
Lachey, Andrew
birth, 18
childhood, 17, 18-20
education, 19-20
as part of 98°, 33-56
joins Just Us, 31-33
Lachey, John, 16, 17-18,
27, 40
Lachey, Lea Dellecave,
52, 53
Lachey, Nicholas Scott
birth, 16
childhood, 16-18, 20
education, 15-16, 18
as part of 98°, 33-56
joins Just Us, 26-33
Lewiston-Porter High
School, 8-11
Lippmann, Jonathan,
26-31
McFayden, Brian, 51
Motown Records, 30,
35, 36-37, 39, 41, 43
MTV, 14, 42, 44, 49,
50-51
Mulan (film), 39-40
"My Everything" (song),
51, 52
"My Name Is" (song), 42
New Edition, 30-31

New Kids on the Block,
28
Nickelodeon All That
Music & More
Festival, 42
98°
albums, 36, 37, 40-41,
42, 43-44, 45, 47,
48-52
formation of, 25-28,
31-33
and High School
Spirit contest, 7-11
as Just Us, 28-33
and *Mulan*, 39-40
name change, 33
recording contract, 35
songs, 10-11, 36, 37,
38, 39-40, 41, 42,
43, 49, 51, 52, 53
and television, 14, 42,
44, 49-52, 53-54
and Top 40
Entertainment, 31,
47
videos, 36, 40, 41, 49,
53
move to Universal
Records, 43
website, 13
98° (album), 36, 37, 47
98° and Rising (album),
40-41, 42, 47
98°: The Official Book, 18
98° Worldwide Fan
Club, 54
'N'Sync, 38, 42
People magazine, 16

60

PolyGram Records, 43
Revelation (album), 48-52
This Christmas (album), 43-44, 47
Timmons, Alyssa, 48
Timmons, Jeffrey Brandon
   birth, 20
   childhood, 20-23
   education, 22-13, 25
   as part of Just Us, 25-33
   as part of 98°, 33-56
Timmons, Jim, 20
Timmons, Patricia, 20, 22
Top 40 Entertainment, 31, 47
Total Request Live (television show), 49, 52, 53
Trackmasters, 41
"True to Your Heart" (song), 39-40, 41
Universal Records, 43, 44, 48
VH-1, 42
"Way You Want Me To, The" (song), 52
"Where You Are" (song), 53
WKSE radio station, 7-9, 36, 56
Wonder, Stevie, 13, 20, 35, 39-40
Z-100 FM radio station, 49-50

Photo Credits:

2: Anthony Cutajar/London Features Int'l
6: Ilpo Musto/London Features Int'l
9: Lisa Rose/Globe Photos
12: W. Cody/Corbis
14: Anthony Cutajar/London Features Int'l
17: Anthony Cutajar/London Features Int'l
19: Anthony Cutajar/London Features Int'l
21: Anthony Cutajar/London Features Int'l
24: Jen Lowery/London Features Int'l
27: Walter Weissman/Globe Photos
29: Jen Lowery/London Features Int'l
32: Jen Lowery/London Features Int'l
34: Ilpo Musto/London Features Int'l
38: Anthony Cutajar/London Features Int'l
43: Henry McGee/Globe Photos
44: Jen Lowery/London Features Int'l
46: Anthony Cutajar/London Features Int'l
50: Andrea Renault/Globe Photos
55: Ron Wolfson/London Features Int'l

Cover photo: Anthony Cutajar/London Features Int'l

About the Author

A native of Buffalo, New York, TIM O'SHEI began writing professionally for sports magazines at age 16. In the eight years since then, he has covered the National Hockey League, the National Football League, and the National Basketball Association, plus written children's books on sports, history, music, and recreation. He was assisted on this book by two talented young writers, Michelle McNamara and Cara Nadrowski.

Ft. Zumwalt West Middle School
150 Waterford Crossing
O'Fallon, MO 63366